The Library of Intergenerational Learning
Native Americans™

Blackfoot Children and Elders Talk Together

E. Barrie Kavasch

The Rosen Publishing Group's
PowerKids Press™
New York

To the Blackfoot People in Canada and the United States, with respect for their amazing history and bright future!

Special appreciation to the Head-Smashed-In Buffalo Jump Museum and Interpretive Center in Fort MacLeod, Alberta, Canada.

Published in 1999 by The Rosen Publishing Group, Inc.
29 East 21st Street, New York, NY 10010

First Edition

Book Design: Danielle Primiceri

Photo Credits: Cover and all inside photos by A. J. Group, John Bacolo.

Kavasch, E. Barrie.
    Blackfoot children and elders talk together/by E. Barrie Kavasch.
        p.   cm.—(Library of intergenerational learning. Native Americans)
    Summary: Explores the culture and traditions of the Blackfoot people through the voices
of some children and elders who are trying to maintain the customs of the past.
    ISBN 0-8239-5228-2
    1. Siksika Indians—History—Juvenile literature. 2. Siksika Indians—Social life and customs—Juvenile literature.
[1. Siksika Indians. 2. Indians of North America.] I. Title. II. Series:
Kavasch, E. Barrie. Library of intergenerational learning. Native Americans.
E99.S54K39 1998
973'.04973—dc21   98-11834
                                                                          CIP
                                                                           AC

Manufactured in the United States of America

Contents

I Am Blackfoot

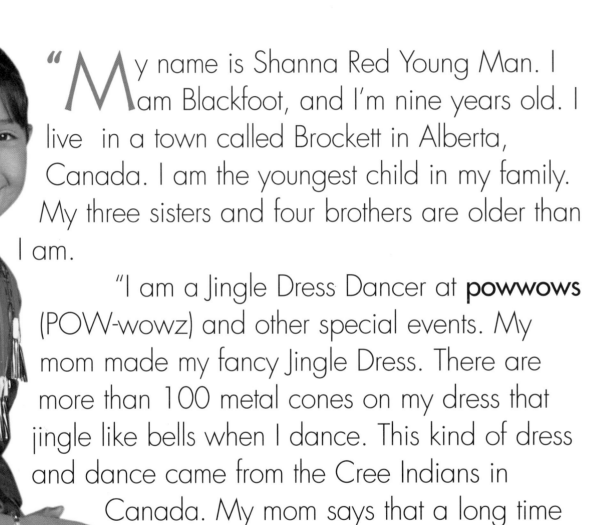

"My name is Shanna Red Young Man. I am Blackfoot, and I'm nine years old. I live in a town called Brockett in Alberta, Canada. I am the youngest child in my family. My three sisters and four brothers are older than I am.

"I am a Jingle Dress Dancer at **powwows** (POW-wowz) and other special events. My mom made my fancy Jingle Dress. There are more than 100 metal cones on my dress that jingle like bells when I dance. This kind of dress and dance came from the Cree Indians in Canada. My mom says that a long time ago it was a part of a Cree Healing

Some say that the name "Blackfoot" comes from a time when the Blackfoot blackened their moccasins with the charcoal and ashes from their cooking fires.

Ceremony (SEHR-eh-mohn-ee)."

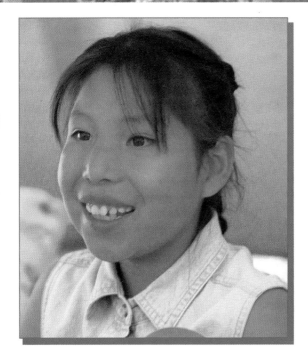

The Blackfoot are called Blackfoot in Canada and Blackfeet in the United States. They are the native people of the northwestern plains of the United States. There are three main related Blackfoot **bands** (BANDZ): the *Siksika*, or Blackfoot, the *Kainah*, or Blood, and the *Pikuni*, or Piegans.

Just as in the past, the Blackfoot continue to **honor** (ON-er) their **culture** (KUL-cher) and **traditions** (truh-DIH-shunz). The children are always learning their Blackfoot language and history from their families, in schools, and on their **reservations** (reh-zer-VAY-shunz). More than 14,500 Blackfeet people live in the United States and over 12,000 Blackfoot people live in Canada.

An Elder Speaks

"I learned my Blackfoot language at home," says Louise Red Young Man. She is Shanna's grandmother. "We only speak Blackfoot, but I understand and speak some English too. Our own language sounds so beautiful.

"Elders are important in Blackfoot culture. We try to keep our future connected with our past through our traditions. I like to talk about the old ways when our **ancestors** (AN-ses-terz) lived in **tipis** (TEE-PEEZ) and hunted the buffalo. They slept on soft buffalo **hides** (HYDZ), and wore buffalo robes. They used a buffalo horn for a drinking cup, and buffalo **dung** (DUNG) was burned in a campfire to keep warm. The people combed their long hair with their fingers. Then they would rub a little bit of buffalo grease into it to make it shine. My grandparents used to live this way."

◀ *Louise Red Young Man often tells her granddaughter, Shanna, about Blackfoot history. She hopes that one day Shanna will tell her children about their people.*

Our Ways

Dion White Man is also Blackfoot. "I like my culture and the Blackfoot spiritual life," he says. "My grandfather, George White Man, was a great dancer. He taught me to dance and to honor my traditions. My great-grandparents gave us a lot of love. They also taught us about **responsibility** (re-spon-sih-BIL-ih-tee).

"After school I like to help my father on the farm. This can be hard work, but I don't mind. I like to work with my dad. And I like to work on the land."

Shirley Bruised Head has worked at the Blackfoot Museum for five years. "I work on educational programs and in our library," says Shirley. "Our **clans** (KLANZ) were once very important. Today the clan **system** (SIS-tem) is disappearing. The smallpox and measels **epidemics** (ep-eh-DEM-iks) of the last hundred years killed many families. That changed many things, including the clans."

This photo shows Dion and his grandfather, George White Man, in Standoff, Alberta, where they live. ▶

Celebrations

"Our biggest celebration is the Sundance gathering," says Shirley. "This event happens every year. It's a very spiritual time. We pray and give thanks to the sun and our Creator, Napi.

"Our culture once centered around the buffalo and our tipis. We followed the buffalo and other big animals that we hunted for food and clothing. We honored the sun and the animals in our Sundance each year.

Some traditional Blackfoot clothing, such as this outfit worn by Charity Many Guns, displays important tribe symbols.

We still do this today. We also celebrate the Buffalo Days Powwow for three days each July.

"Today we make traditional clothes to wear for celebrations. Feather fans and fancy hats and shawls with long, silky fringe are worn and carried by many of the women dancers. They wear breast plates and necklaces of fine shell beads. Some of the women have elk teeth sewn on their finest dresses. Our dance clothes show important **symbols** (SIM-bulz) in our lives."

Blackfoot clothes show a respect for the land and the Blackfoot way of life. ▶

11

An Elder's Story

Blackfoot elders are respected. The elders teach the younger **generations** (jen-er-AY-shunz) about Blackfoot history and the ways of life. The Blackfoot have many stories about Napi, or Old Man. Napi created the land and everything on it.

Napi made the mountains, prairies, and all things out of mud and clay. He worked very hard until he got everything just right. Napi created things to fly in the air and others to crawl under the earth. It took him four days just to make the first people. He called them the *Siksika*. Napi taught them how to make weapons and to hunt for their food. He even let the people make their own choices about life and death so they would learn to care about each other.

There are many stories about Blackfoot Indian history. These are early lessons in Blackfoot culture. Some of the stories are very funny. The elders believe it is important to learn but also to laugh.

◀ *Respected elders, such as Tom Crane Bear of the* Siksika, *respect the importance of Blackfoot stories as part of Blackfoot history.*

The Land

Blackfoot land stretches across high rolling plains. It is divided into seven areas in Alberta, Canada, and the Blackfoot reservation in northern Montana. The land ends at the Rocky Mountains. The Blackfoot call these mountains "the backbone of the world." Blackfoot homelands once stretched much farther, from Canada to the northwestern United States.

There are some beautiful areas on Blackfoot land. There are **sacred** (SAY-kred) places where the Blackfoot people go on personal journeys. Even the rocks seem to have special power. The Blackfoot people have lived in these regions for thousands of years.

Historical Blackfoot land can be seen along one of the trails of the Blackfoot museum, or the Head-Smashed-In Buffalo Jump Interpretive Center. ▶

Families

"I enjoy sewing and making new dance outfits for my daughters," says Doreen Red Young Man. "I also make their leggings and dance moccasins. My mother, Louise, taught me a lot of our traditional crafts.

"I study with other Blackfoot elders who teach us more about our language and crafts. These classes are held during the week at our Piegan Community Elders Center. Next week I'm going to a sweat lodge rite of **purification** (pyer-if-ih-KAY-shun). An elder will be leading this for us."

Families are an important part of Blackfoot culture. They help each other learn about their important history and prepare for their futures.

Four generations of the Red Young Man family can be seen here. Doreen holds her granddaughter, Kelly (left). Her brothers, Robert and Phillip, stand behind Shanna and Louise Red Young Man.

Ceremonies

"The Buffalo Jump Celebration is my favorite event," says Shanna. "We all gather near the museum and put up our tipis. We have a tipi village because there are so many of us.

Also, there are so many gophers around that you have to watch out for gopher holes. The other night a gopher came into our tipi! But he didn't stay!"

The Blackfoot celebrate many things in life, but their **heritage** (HEHR-ih-tij) is the **foundation** (fown-DAY-shun) of their culture. The finest dancers carry flags as they prepare to lead everyone into the dance circle. But first a respected elder carries the Eagle Staff onto the dance grounds to bless the ceremony. The leader always carries the Eagle Staff with great pride.

Many Blackfoot on the reservation participate in the Buffalo Jump Celebration. It is a big event for everyone. ▶

Food and Prayers

"I like pizza and hamburgers and soda, especially at school and at powwows," says Shanna. "But my favorite food is my Mom's homemade cabbage rolls. She makes the very best!"

"Our traditional meats were buffalo, moose, elk, and deer," says Shirley Bruised Head. "These were dried and made into a food called **pemmican** (PEM-ih-kan). One favorite dessert is Saskatoon Pie. It is made in the summer when Saskatoon berries are ripe. These delicious berries make a very purple pie. Many Blackfoot enjoy it during the summer.

"Prayers are another important part of our culture. Our prayers are usually spoken in our Blackfoot language. Elders offer their prayers at the beginning of powwows and other celebrations. We pray for our friends and families. We offer our prayers to the sun for gifts of life, friends, and family."

Blackfoot culture is often a part of everyday life for Shanna and her family. Here, Shanna enjoys a buffalo burger for lunch. ▶

The last few hundred years have been difficult for the Blackfoot. But the Blackfoot have hope for their children, who are their future. Blackfoot elders hope that the children will respect themselves and each other.

The elders tell this to their children: "Look back to the ways of our great-grandparents. Look how they lived and learned from life. Look after our young women, who were always considered the center of our universe. Our young men need to take care of themselves and be responsible. We have great hopes for you and for our culture."

Glossary

ancestor (AN-ses-ter) A relative who lived long before you.

band (BAND) A smaller group within an Indian tribe.

ceremony (SEHR-eh-mohn-ee) A special activity done at a certain time.

clan (KLAN) A group of people who are related within a tribe.

culture (KUL-cher) The beliefs, customs, art, and religions of a group of people.

dung (DUNG) Animal waste.

epidemic (ep-eh-DEM-ik) The quick spreading of a disease so that many people have it at the same time.

foundation (fown-DAY-shun) The strong part on which other parts are built.

generation (jen-er-AY-shun) People born in the same period of time.

heritage (HEHR-ih-tij) The cultural traditions that are handed down from parent to child.

hide (HYD) The skin of an animal.

honor (ON-er) To show admiration and respect.

pemmican (PEM-ih-kan) Concentrated dried meat, fat, and fruits pressed together.

powwow (POW-wow) A special Native American festival of events and gatherings.

purification (pyer-if-ih-KAY-shun) To make something pure, or very clean.

reservation (reh-zer-VAY-shun) An area of land set aside by the government for Indians to live on.

responsibility (re-spon-sih-BIL-ih-tee) Something that a person must take care of or complete.

sacred (SAY-kred) Something that is very important and highly respected.

symbol (SIM-bul) A design that stands for something else.

system (SIS-tem) An orderly way of getting things done.

tipi (TEE-PEE) A triangular home made of animal skin and wood.

tradition (truh-DIH-shun) To do things the same way that a group of people has done them for a long time.

Index